Gretzky's Game

by
Mike Leonetti

illustrations by
Greg Banning

Scholastic Canada Ltd.
Toronto New York London Auckland Sydney
Mexico City New Delhi Hong Kong Buenos Aires

ACKNOWLEDGEMENTS
The author used the following reference materials: books by these writers: Jack Canfield (editor),
Michael Boughn, John Davidson, Stan Fischler, Walter Gretzky, Wayne Gretzky, Kevin Lowe,
Terry Jones, Rick Reilly, Sherry Ross, Jeff Rud, Jim Taylor and Barry Wilner. Magazines and newspapers:
Sports Illustrated, *The Hockey News*, *NHL Powerplay*, *Maclean's*, Edmonton Oilers game programs
from the 1983–84 season, *The Calgary Herald*, the *Toronto Star*. Statistical reference guides:
NHL Guide and Record Book, *Total NHL*, *2004 World Cup Guide*. Film: *Hockey Night in Canada* game
broadcast of May 19, 1984; *A&E Biography: Wayne Gretzky*.

The author wishes to thank the staff at Raincoast Books for all their efforts, and especially editor Scott
Steedman, who was of great help in developing this story.

Scholastic Canada Ltd.
604 King Street West, Toronto, Ontario M5V 1E1, Canada

Scholastic Inc.
557 Broadway, New York, NY 10012, USA

Scholastic Australia Pty Limited
PO Box 579, Gosford, NSW 2250, Australia

Scholastic New Zealand Limited
Private Bag 94407, Botany, Manukau 2163, New Zealand

Scholastic Children's Books
Euston House, 24 Eversholt Street, London NW1 1DB, UK

Library and Archives Canada Cataloguing in Publication
Leonetti, Mike, 1958-
Gretzky's game / by Mike Leonetti ; illustrations by
Greg Banning.

ISBN 978-1-4431-0729-7

1. Gretzky, Wayne, 1961- --Juvenile fiction.
2. Edmonton Oilers (Hockey team)--Juvenile fiction.
I. Banning, Greg II. Title.

PS8573.E58734G74 2011   jC813'.54   C2011-902071-8

6 5 4 3 2 1   Printed in Singapore 46   11 12 13 14 15

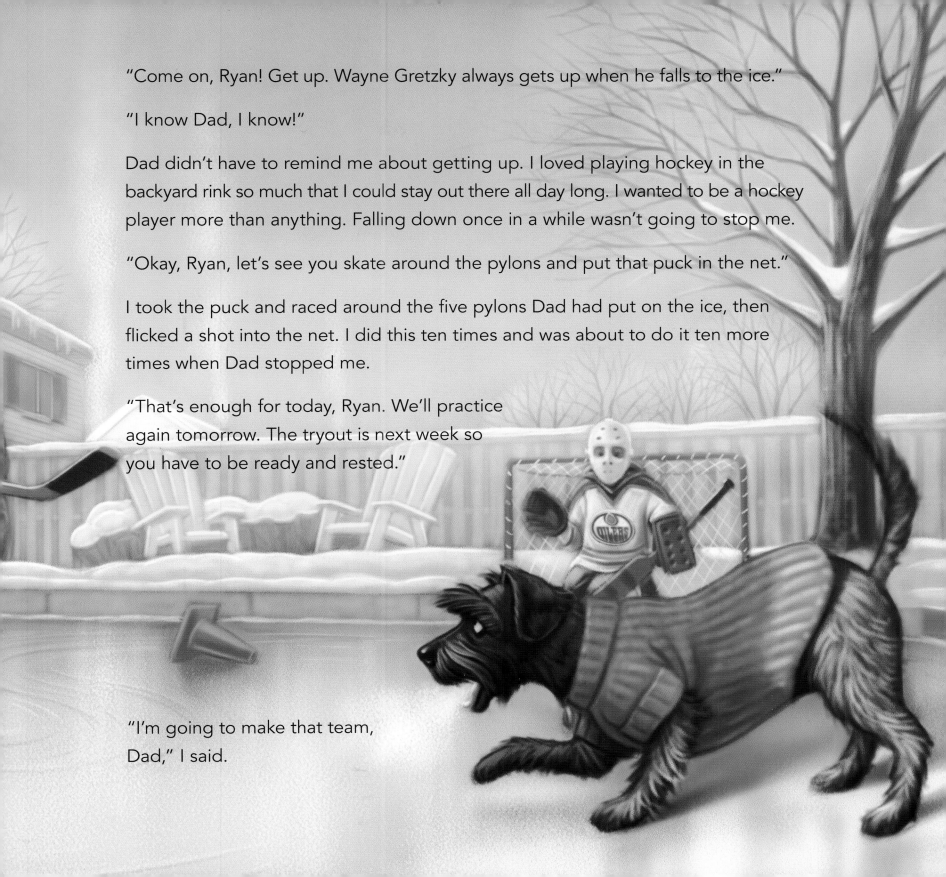

"Come on, Ryan! Get up. Wayne Gretzky always gets up when he falls to the ice."

"I know Dad, I know!"

Dad didn't have to remind me about getting up. I loved playing hockey in the backyard rink so much that I could stay out there all day long. I wanted to be a hockey player more than anything. Falling down once in a while wasn't going to stop me.

"Okay, Ryan, let's see you skate around the pylons and put that puck in the net."

I took the puck and raced around the five pylons Dad had put on the ice, then flicked a shot into the net. I did this ten times and was about to do it ten more times when Dad stopped me.

"That's enough for today, Ryan. We'll practice again tomorrow. The tryout is next week so you have to be ready and rested."

"I'm going to make that team, Dad," I said.

I had been a house league player for a couple of years, but next week I was going to try out for a select team called the Oil Kings. It was going to be a challenge for me because of my size. I'm not as tall or as heavy as most other boys my age. My hockey sweaters are always too big on me and my hockey pants sort of droop down, which makes people think I'm too small to play with bigger kids. But I have been skating since I was two years old, so I can move around the ice pretty well. I practice hard to develop my passing and puck-handling skills. My dad told me I have to be faster and smarter than the bigger boys, so I work at hockey every chance I get so that I can get better.

It's really easy for me to practice hockey every day. As soon as it gets cold enough, Dad gets my younger brother Jason and me to help him put up the boards and flood the backyard. We skate every day on our very own rink before and after school. On the weekends we have our friends over and play hockey all day long.

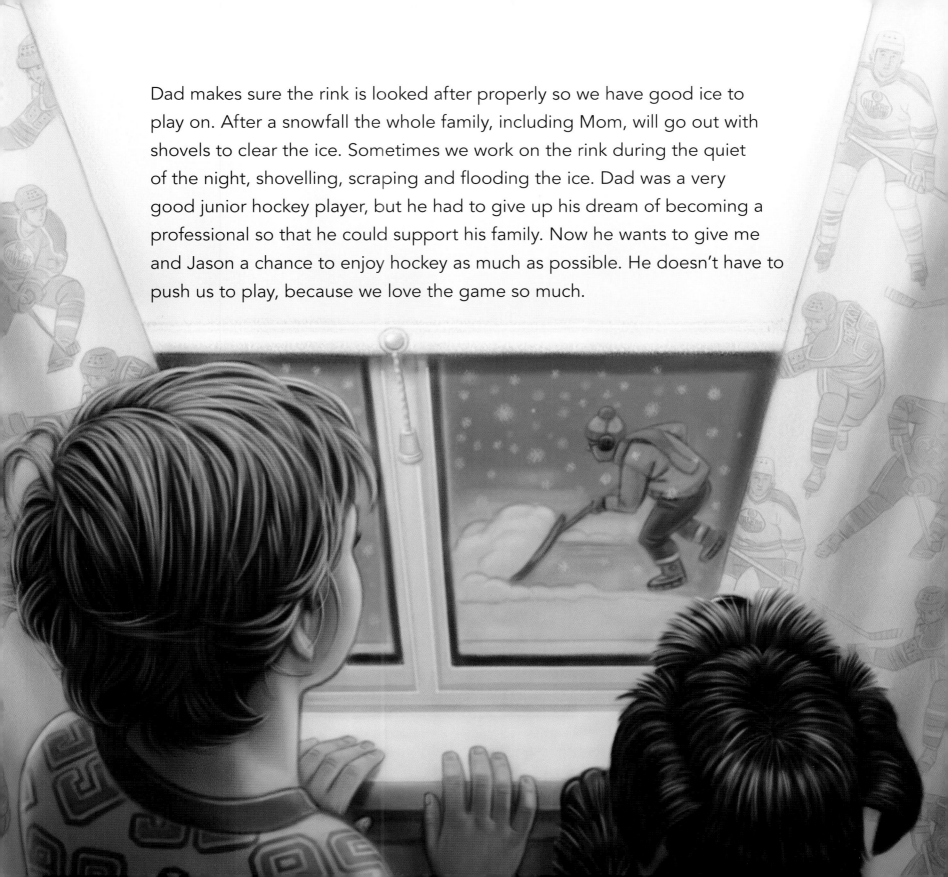

Dad makes sure the rink is looked after properly so we have good ice to play on. After a snowfall the whole family, including Mom, will go out with shovels to clear the ice. Sometimes we work on the rink during the quiet of the night, shovelling, scraping and flooding the ice. Dad was a very good junior hockey player, but he had to give up his dream of becoming a professional so that he could support his family. Now he wants to give me and Jason a chance to enjoy hockey as much as possible. He doesn't have to push us to play, because we love the game so much.

There was one last roster spot to fill on the Oil Kings and coach Bodnar was looking for a keen player to add to his squad. Dad had managed to convince the coach to give me a tryout. This was my chance to show that I had what it takes to play on a select team.

I did all sorts of drills to prepare for the tryout. Jason played in net so that I would have a goalie to shoot against. I worked hard at my skating and at moving the puck quickly so that I could avoid getting hit.

"Ryan, I want you to do your best, but don't be too disappointed if you don't make the team. The coach might think you're too small, so you'll have to impress him with your skills and your smarts. I know how excited you are by this, but your mother and I are still not sure if you're ready for it right now," Dad said.

"Dad, they used to tell Wayne Gretzky that he was too small, and that he would never make the NHL. Look at him now!" I said.

Wayne Gretzky was my favourite player. He was captain of the Edmonton Oilers, my hometown team. Many people had told him he was too small and slight and that his shot was too weak to make it in professional hockey, but he had sure proved them wrong. When he first joined the NHL at age eighteen, they said he was too young, but he scored 51 goals and got 86 assists and won the most valuable player award! One year he scored 92 goals and got 212 points. He had already recorded over 100 assists in a season three times, and was breaking record after record.

I had started keeping a scrapbook on Gretzky and any time I felt that I couldn't do something, I'd take it out and go through it carefully.

"GRETZKY FILLS RINK AND THE NET"

"OILERS UPSET MIGHTY MONTREAL CANADIENS"

"GRETZKY SHATTERS NHL RECORD"

"FIRST PLAYER TO RECORD OVER 200 POINTS"

"GRETZKY GETS 50 WITH FIVE-GOAL NIGHT"

These were just some of the headlines in my scrapbook.

I made sure I had a Titan brand hockey stick just like Gretzky. If the best player in hockey used that stick, I figured it would be good enough for me! I bought an Oilers sweater with number 99, Gretzky's number, on the back. I had Gretzky posters in my room, and a Gretzky ruler for school. At breakfast I ate my cereal from a box with a picture of Wayne on it. He was the reason I was so interested in hockey, and I didn't want to forget that for even one minute!

On the day of my tryout I was nervous, and I really wanted to do well. Coach Bodnar skated over to me and said, "Hi, Ryan. Are you ready to go?"

"Yes sir," I said, trying to sound as confident as I could.

"Good. Now here's what I am looking for from you," he said, and he showed me the paper on his clipboard. I would be tested on my skating ability and speed, hitting targets on the net, and moving through an obstacle course. There were two other categories on the sheet. One was "hockey smarts" and the other was "desire."

I skated my hardest and tried to remember all the things I'd been practising. When it was all over, coach Bodnar talked things through with my dad. Then he skated over to me.

"Ryan, I really like your desire and you seem to understand the game pretty well. I'm concerned about how you will handle the rough play, because you're smaller than most of the boys. But you have good skills so I've decided to give you a spot on the team as our third or fourth centre."

"All right!" I screamed out loud and jumped up in the air. I was so happy. I had always wanted to play centre just like my hero, Wayne Gretzky.

"Ryan, I know you're thrilled about this, but I don't know how much ice time you're going to get in games. I want you to be careful along the boards and in front of the net. You can learn to handle the physical play with practice, and we'll see how you do."

"I understand, Coach."

I learned so much about hockey by watching Gretzky play on television or when my Dad took Jason and me to games at Northlands Coliseum. Sometimes I would go and watch the Oilers practise when my mom took us shopping at West Edmonton Mall. The team practised on a rink there and we loved to sit in the stands and watch our heroes in action. I could see what a hard worker Gretzky was, even at practice. He was always trying new moves and seemed so dedicated to improving, even though he was already the best player in the league. You could see that he just loved to play hockey — it was his game!

The Oilers were having another great season, and Gretzky began the year with at least one point in 51 straight games to set another record. In one game against the Minnesota North Stars, Gretzky got eight points — four goals and four assists — and the Oilers won 12–8! It looked like Edmonton would finish on top of the league.

I kept trying to become a better player by practising all the time. I was good at setting up plays and could make long tape-to-tape passes to spring my wingers for a chance to score. But I didn't get much ice time during games. I tried hard every chance I got but I still hadn't scored a goal, and a centre needs to score. I wanted a goal very badly, but I was sort of afraid to stand in front of the net where I could get whacked or pushed around.

I was sad about not scoring even one goal. I felt like I wasn't helping the team. Mom noticed that I was unhappy one day when she picked me up from practice.

"What's the problem, Ryan?"

"I haven't done much to help the team win. I don't even have a goal yet," I said. I had to fight to stop from crying.

"Well, I don't know much about hockey, Ryan, but it seems to me that you have to shoot to score," Mom said. "Practise your shot more. That might work."

Maybe Mom wasn't a hockey expert, but her idea made a lot of sense.

"Thanks, Mom, that really helps."

The next day I was out practising on the backyard rink and Dad set up four targets on the corners of the net. With Dad feeding me passes, I tried to hit the targets starting at ten feet out and then moving further back. I didn't have a hard shot but it was quick and accurate, and I managed to hit the targets and get a few past Jason in net. I practised like this every chance I got, and I started to get better at scoring from further out. I began to feel like I knew how to score! Now I just had to do it during a game!

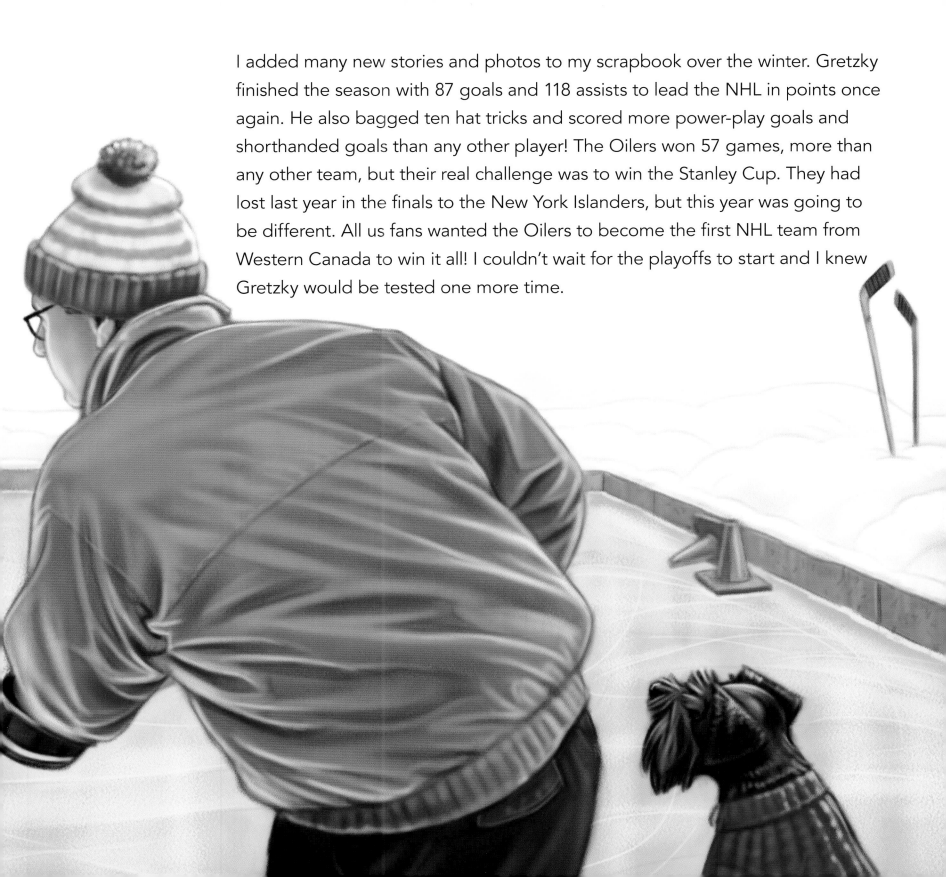

I added many new stories and photos to my scrapbook over the winter. Gretzky finished the season with 87 goals and 118 assists to lead the NHL in points once again. He also bagged ten hat tricks and scored more power-play goals and shorthanded goals than any other player! The Oilers won 57 games, more than any other team, but their real challenge was to win the Stanley Cup. They had lost last year in the finals to the New York Islanders, but this year was going to be different. All us fans wanted the Oilers to become the first NHL team from Western Canada to win it all! I couldn't wait for the playoffs to start and I knew Gretzky would be tested one more time.

Before my team's final game of the season, the captain came over and sat beside me in the dressing room. Michael was our best player and had scored lots of goals. He was like a magician with the puck, shooting and passing so smoothly.

"Listen, Ryan. When you get a chance, try to skate between the face-off circles in the other team's end. As soon as the pass hits your stick, let it go. I've seen you do it in practice and you have a good shot." I just nodded.

I didn't play much early in the game, but I had a few good shifts when I did get on. The coach seemed to have more confidence in me so he played me more even though we were losing 3–2. Late in the game, Michael was on a shift with me, and I passed him the puck. He raced toward the other team's zone, whizzing past two defenders. I saw what was happening and headed for the right spot, just like he had told me to. As soon as I was in position, Michael sent me a pass. I saw the puck coming and as soon as it hit my stick, I shot as quickly as I could. The puck sailed over the goalie's shoulder and into the net. GOAL!

My teammates jumped on the ice and congratulated me. It was my only goal of the season and it tied the game!

Edmonton had breezed past the Winnipeg Jets in the first round of the playoffs but had a much harder time against the Calgary Flames. The Oilers finally won the series in seven games and then they beat Minnesota in four. Edmonton was back in the finals just like they had hoped, and once again they would play the Islanders for the Stanley Cup!

The Oilers won the first game 1–0, but the Islanders won the next one 6–1. I didn't mind losing one game, because my Dad and I had tickets for the fifth game of the series, which was going to be played in Edmonton. The Oilers wiped the Islanders out in the next two games, winning both by a score of 7–2. One more win and the Cup would belong to Edmonton!

Gretzky was having a bit of a hard time against the Islanders. He hadn't got a single goal in the finals last year and hadn't scored once in the first three games this year. People said that Bryan Trottier of the Islanders was a better player and leader. But Gretzky kept his cool, and in the fourth game he scored the opening goal on a breakaway. It was a big relief for him, but a lot of people still wondered if he was ready to fulfill his lifelong dream and take his team to the Cup. I was sure the Oilers would win because they had so many great players like Mark Messier, Paul Coffey, Jari Kurri, Kevin Lowe, Glenn Anderson, and Grant Fuhr and Andy Moog in goal! But I knew that Gretzky would have to lead the way.

We got to the Coliseum early for the game. I wore my Oilers sweater for good luck. Dad had managed to get great seats right near centre ice between the team benches. The Oilers got a loud standing ovation when they took the ice. Many people had painted or drawn signs and they were hung around the arena. "Bury them, Oilers!" said one. "Sink the Islanders!" urged another, and my favourite one simply said, "Go for It!"

Andy Moog was playing in net for the Oilers and he made some great saves early on in the game. The Islanders seemed determined to win this game and send the series back to New York. They were going for five straight Cups and were not going to give up without a hard fight.

Then, halfway through the first period, Kurri sprung Gretzky into the clear with a great pass. Number 99 flew down the wing, cut across the middle of the ice past an Islander defenceman and slid a shot under goalie Billy Smith. 1–0 for the Oilers! The arena exploded in celebration.

Five minutes later, Edmonton broke up a play at the blue line and three Oilers rushed down the ice with only one New York player back. Kurri passed it to Gretzky in the centre. The Oilers captain kept skating and looked up to see if he should shoot or pass. He decided to let one go and buried a shot right between the goalie's pads. 2–0!

Gretzky was showing everyone that he could play his best when it mattered most. You could see how badly he wanted to win the Cup!

In the second period, the Oilers scored two more to make it 4–0. It seemed like the game was all wrapped up, but the Islanders were champs and they were not going to quit. Pat LaFontaine scored two goals just 34 seconds apart to start the third period and give the Islanders some hope. The score was 4–2 and everyone was a little nervous. The Oilers tightened up and Moog made some more good saves to keep Edmonton up by two.

Suddenly it was the last minute of play and the Islanders pulled their goalie for an extra attacker. The crowd was standing and cheering when the puck came out to Dave Lumley in the Edmonton end. He spun and took a long shot that ended up right in the middle of the empty New York net. 5–2 for the Oilers and only 12 seconds to go!

The fans started a countdown with eight seconds to go.

Four . . . three . . . two . . . one . . .

It was all over! Everyone mobbed Moog at the end of the rink and the crowd was going wild. The Stanley Cup was brought out and placed on a table at centre ice. Gretzky skated over and when the Cup was handed to him, he smiled so big! He lifted the Cup over his head as teammates swarmed around him. He could barely move through the crowd of people on the ice, but you could see how happy and proud he was.

I turned to my Dad and shouted, "He did it again!"

"Yep, he sure proved himself tonight," Dad replied. "That's what great players do. Did you see the way he skated? He wasn't going to let anyone stop him."

"I'm never going to forget this moment," I said happily.

During the summer I drank lots of milk and took my vitamins. I also played a lot of street hockey and worked on my shot. I grew a little taller and heavier, and I made the select team early in the fall. I was no longer afraid of going in front of the net, just like Gretzky had done in the finals. In the first game of the season I had a chance to score on a breakaway. I skated hard like Gretzky always did, and the big defenceman trying to stop my rush couldn't catch me. The goalie went for a fake and I went around him before putting a shot into the net. It was the kind of goal Wayne Gretzky would score. If I keep working on my game just like Gretzky does, I might win the Stanley Cup one day, too!

About Wayne Gretzky

Wayne Gretzky was born in Brantford, Ontario, in 1961 and by the time he was eleven years old he was already a hockey star. In the 1971–72 season he scored 378 goals and recorded 120 assists in 85 games with his local team. By the age of seventeen he was playing professional hockey in the World Hockey Association, and he graduated to the National Hockey League when the Edmonton Oilers joined the circuit in 1979. He won four Stanley Cups with the Oilers and took the Art Ross Trophy as the league's leading scorer ten times. He also won the Lady Byng Trophy for gentlemanly play on five occasions and the Conn Smythe for the best player in the playoffs twice. He was traded to the Los Angeles Kings in 1988 in one of the biggest trades in sports history. Gretzky also played for the St. Louis Blues and the New York Rangers before he retired in 1999. He finished his remarkable career the holder of 61 NHL records, including most career goals (894), assists (1,963) and points (2,857) and most goals (122), assists (260) and points (382) in the playoffs. His sweater number 99 has been retired by the entire NHL. Gretzky became part-owner of the Phoenix Coyotes in 2000 and coached them from 2004 to 2009. He also served as Executive Director of the Canadian team that won the Olympics (2002) and the World Cup of Hockey (2004). For hockey fans, he will always be remembered as "The Great One."